IN THE WELLSPRING OF THE EAR

IN THE WELLSPRING OF THE EAR

Poems New & Selected

Tomas O'Leary

LYNX HOUSE PRESS
Spokane, Washington

Acknowledgments

Previous journal publication of these poems include appearances in *Agora, Anathema, Arion's Dolphin, Bagel Bard Anthologies* (1 thru 10), *The Blacksmith, Cambridge Chronicle, Choice, The Chowder Review, Colorado Review, Cow Creek Review, Cutthroat, East Coast Poets, Hubbub, Ibbetson Street, Lynx, Midwest Quarterly, Mississippi Mud, Muddy River Poetry Review, Niagara, Pittsburg* (MA) *Eagle, Pomegranate Press* (broadside), *North River Press* (broadside), *Ploughshares, Poiesis, Royal Gazette* (Bermuda), *Scarab, Somerville* (MA) *News, Spare Change, Spectrum, Street Magazine, Stringtown, Willow Springs, Wilderness House Literary Review, The Worcester Review, Words,* and *Working from Silence.*

Many of the poems included also appeared in the following full-length volumes:

Fool at the Funeral (Lynx House Press, 1975)
The Devil Take a Crooked House (Lynx House Press, 1990)
A Prayer for Everyone (Ilora Press, 2010)

Project Editor: Christopher Howell.
Cover Art: Entre Nous, encaustic by Jeff League, whose work can be viewed at
    http:/jeffleaugue.com/
Author Photo: Lee Post.
Book Design: Christine Holbert.

FIRST EDITION

Cataloging-in-Publication Data available from the Library of Congress.

ISBN: 978-089924-143-2

Contents

III IN FROGGING TIME

for Lee Post, the Photographer, my dear wife
& for Christopher Howell, the Poet & Editor, my dear friend

I

STUCK WITH THE REMAINS

House on the High Road

High lady low road the red treasure
Again on my hands, my intention
I swear was words only
A reasoned package to deliver her,
Therefore I went

My both hands empty and outheld
She could see, she could see
Such innocent bare angles
My thoughts cut
Crossing the last stones

Now the dogs burn for my own blood
Therefore the low road (the high
Is policed by submissions)
This red on my hands I cry
Up to the troubled assemblies

Was words, I swear, was words only!

Portrait of Alvarez

The undertaker Alvarez, virile
in his late fifties, spikes
mortality with the best tequila;
nails down sex and death
saying:
"They are the wings of the wild bird
that bears us far from circumstance."

He has a young blonde wife
and worries
horns upon his head; although she holds
his baby son, and minds
his busy telephone
in the showroom of coffins—
black and long, or white and measured
for a child . . .

Often, in passing, I look in
on Alvarez: he wakes my heart
to a sadness so profound
I feel the pinch of his profession
in my brown shoes. As lonely
keeper of the last door, in this
large mountain pueblo
where death and sex visibly beat the air
with equal frequency, Alvarez
rings his eyes with work,
his sign—in Spanish—shouting:
"Service, Day and Night."

Across the bridge from Alvarez
pigs die all day, their madly human cries
clawing a world of slaughter
whose stucco wall bleeds freely through a pipe
and down the clay bank
to rest—in the rainless season–on the muddy water's edge . . .

And once, in the spell of
Alvarez, as we stood with sunset
on the bridge, I saw
that blood-beast swallow
our day's last bleeding leg of light
into the sluggish stream.

Imaginary Dawn

The matrix of night's dissolution
contracts, and patches of dew
shiver on a stone green hill.

Beyond, in bolting grey,
the first of a band of red horses
has climbed to a cold spine of mountains
and mastered its chill, and now watches.

The moon is unsure of herself,
her children have vanished; she pauses
in her slow, sensible circuit
and searches the lightening blanket.

Now nothing is new or old
or under the thumb of the living
or numb with the gift of the dead;
the face of light assembles:

the limbering, steep ensemble
of atmosphere and roots
soon sharpens the stone's predilection
that light resurrect with a noose,
that the hanged earth resist all equation
with the quick, the loose.

Timestones

Stone monuments instruct the eye
to die, and dream of overkill;
of cash equivalent for flesh;
of better ways to strip the earth
and scrape her veins to force the hour.
All right, then: sculpt me a stone flower.

My father quoted me a line
he couldn't place, but here it is:
"Hope brings a terror to the human heart."
Although I like the sentiment,
his saying it is what I love.
Leave me enough to know I live.

As I count backwards, as these days
defined by death bend out toward death,
blue roses are the numbered row.
The reach of God is nothing new.
Sometimes I own a sense of doom
so wrought, there's dancing in the tomb.

Tell me another, brother Ears—
your spaces will partake of me
before I understand the words
that wish a death on anyone.
(Is life the edge of love's wild guess?
The skilled assassin whispers, *Yes!)*

Stars and their shadows feed us on
into infinity. My strings
will not be eaten by the rats.
The laughing harpist understands

a simple premise: here we are.
Hunger has driven us this far.

Over the aeons, far from now,
the whispering prophets congregate
around the certainty that all
will flower suddenly on earth
as it is in heaven . . .
                              Stones ascend
to orbit the impossible,
                        the end!

Loneliness of the Gladfish Pedlar

Once
when they were out of season
a gladfish pedlar walked our cobbled street
both sides, back and forth
hawking his small treasures . . .

> *Gladfish gladfish*
> *singin' in my pocket,*
> *pay a little money-o*
> *and own a few and off you go*

All day
he rang the alleyways
waiting for the passersby to gather;
all around I followed him
and wished I had a nickel
for a bagful.
His song sailed off at every ear
(gladfish never were in big demand)
but I tagged along
until, turned dead by his burden
and night nearly full,
he limped away toward the sea.

My Father's Song

My father's seed
is the love of song,
he ploughs the void green

forever; yet I find
no trace of him
as the mist lifts, and I stand

aeons away
on a verdant planet,
knee-deep in memory's dung,

minding his song.

None of the Old Familiar

When reasonable men lost ground, in the dense
histories that precede this lie,
a quiet lessening of light was all
the heavens ever answered with, the way
few knew themselves the darker off.

Even those few who knew the pain
the gentle mind must know in failing God,
even they acted out the germ
of empire's loving knowledge of itself,
and trusted worship, though they'd lost the state.

Stirring this loosely into present context,
the token measures that the just man takes
who hears his world has flown apart, do not
suffice to add one candle power
where only death has ever drawn a crowd.

How we adorn the *dream* is all that matters:
the messengers are at their posts
pecking the season to its close.
None of the old familiar serves the land,
whose random saviors murder even ghosts.

Angerthas

The brain of blackest Angerthas
        (the beauty that is no one's cat)
contains a million city miles
        of neon soup and sorcery.

The torrid avenues inveigh
        against all involution,
for the thought must be the deed
        wherever Angerthas perceives
                the demon lurking.

Her life begins and ends at dawn;
        her hours of sleep are silent dogs
that dream of cats that dream of dogs;
        her days are open to the breeze.

She is the bone and hair of night.
        She is the lone one, stretching there.
Her eyes are tunnels to their ends.

Inch down them, loving, if you dare.

Stuck with the Remains

First of all they were blowing
Up the mountain
Rock breath gusting in my face

Thy whiskered saint
Journeying far on foot
Through the badlands, red

Roses pasted on his teeth
A Christian bugle
Frowning from each eye

I was a dog at times
Like that, my body had grown
Its third hand, I felt

Nothing, not the panic
These long walks bestilled
Not the wet kiss of a snake

Or Thy burdensome legs that rode me
All the desert miles.
Sadly I lapsed into thought

And by Thy leave
And with a blessing
Befriended those killers of the mountain

Ordering skins and bones
Archaic hearts and complex
Settlements of sinew and vein

Into Thy lamb-thick junkyard paradise.

At the Wake of Child Called Beauty

They've come to celebrate
with murmured grief and great decorum
the dead and all but buried past
of a young niece, laid out
for their last inspection.

Each must converse with certain ones,
then join the sighing shuffle.
Their argument with death does not disturb
the flushed, familiar face
waiting for morning, a nailed roof, and earth.

But as they crowd the open coffin,
right hands cutting rapid crosses on the air
of their bodies, it is as if
their hearts had leapt like fists
to fill their throats,

for sudden laughter rocks the room!—
an ancient moppet, maybe
a great aunt, or some distant wife,
straining the seams of her paper face,
stunning the proper gloom.

The rush of whisperings as she leans
over the innocence of death . . .
the whirling roses, the receding floor . . .
perfumes and voices mingling in a field
where the child sleeps . . .

Surely, as Beauty lies alive
between two breaths—the out, the in—
the old one hanging on her clean white bed
has found the thread of childhood,
and forgotten death.

The Pleasures of Mourning

Uncle Morris is displayed
in a seersucker suit
having two days before
kicked the bucket
at age seventy-four.

Some less than given
to reverence,
being fifteen and difficult,
I treat the wake as a joke
and sneak a smoke.

It's mostly an old crowd,
and none of them's exactly floored
by Morris's demise—
he was tight with a buck
and had mean eyes.

My brother, who's got this dry wit,
says right in the casket room,
"What's the big attraction here,
Uncle Morris or what?"
My cousin elbows him and says, "You nut!"

Then Father Kelly and fellow reverends
roll in in two cars;
the old boys in the sitting room
snipe our their cigars
and we all kneel down.

We swing right into a rosary,
Our Fathers, Hail Marys, and *Glory Bes*
all sent on up for Morris's sake
figuring, "He'll go to heaven if they take."
It's a lively wake.

There are flowers all over,
and cards about paradise
and how the Lord is good,
and one that says "Hope you're feeling better"
from an aunt who misunderstood.

Cousin Brenda says, "He'd never smile."
Uncle Mike says, "Ah, he was gettin' senile."
Aunt Sarah sighs, "Perhaps it's for the best."
They all agree the rest'll do him good
and that the room is humid.

Frank the Mortician mixes with the mourners,
seeing their tears are under control;
he slaps my dad on the back and says,
"You're lookin' fit for fightin',
bless your soul!"

There are lots of conversations
going around the parlor;
far as I can gather,
they're about taxes and politics
and what's the matter.

Well, it goes on like it'll never end;
but then around nine-thirty the crowd thins
and even the hang-ons are out by ten—
except for Uncle Morris,
and he don't know he's been.

And Frank's staying on awhile too.
I can see him through the window
whistling some undertaker's tune
and doing a little soft shoe.
And the lights go off.

My Father, My Sons

A genius at blather, a serious man to boot
was my father, now decades buried.
I'd like to steal up on him and shout
bold love, as a fact unworried.

Being Irish we lavish affection
in cryptic ways we dare not scrutinize,
lest our innocence worm towards corruption
as the heart revealed draws flies.

He died it seems almost forever ago,
yet here he is to tell me this:
"Sure eternity doesn't take but a day,
and day turns to day, and nothing ever missed."

He had a thousand Irish songs
entirely in his memory, and he gave them voice
that filled with joy their hopeless longings,
failed rebellions, centuries of loss.

I was not raised to speak of love;
obliqueness keeps our full hearts from exploding.
Enough to say, "You make me glad
of all that's near or distant, yet unfolding."

My sons, alive and well, have never met
the old man who was father to their old man,
the mythic fish who barely missed their net.
He's theirs, though, surely as he's mine.

I'd have them know the bridge is in the saying,
the crossing over simple, dreamt, unsaid.
As memory is the bed of all our risings,
I'd love their odd word, though I'm decades dead.

Quantum Meat Chant

The house is heavy
We are dead with waiting
Where is our meat
We are dead with waiting
We would sing
But we are out of songs
We have ordered meat
We are dead with waiting

Do not awaken us
We are dead with waiting
When you come with our meat
We do not eat meat
And are dead with waiting
And are done with waiting
And do not eat meat
And did not order meat

Yet you have come
We are eating meat
Who were dead with waiting
And are dead with eating
And must leave our bodies
Leaning in their seats
Over meat
They have eaten
Waiting

Waking Up Naked on Mother's Day

I used to wake up in my clothes
in ditches by the sides of roads
and walk all morning before coming
to. For talk I would recite my name
and name each thing I saw, and introduce them
name to name. Sometimes a town
that had gone under would line up
both sides of me and scare a hole
through my bowels. The medicine
man, more wisp than flesh, would fish
me from my shallow sleep and mumble me
cursed but cured. So much
fell out. So all falls out . . .

If I feel pain my mother's womb is
vacant where I voted No. There's
there to go, as there's a grave
or a green bush to lie in. That now
I wake up in the raw, retch,
curse my teeth and call it bust
is just one kind of morning, mom.
I'm an old road-seasoned soldier
taking his licks, licking his wounds
and sometimes even salting them
for visions, or for kicks . . .

Am I off my feed, am I in debt?
The way I read that bathroom scale there is
no safe eternity. And here's
the kicker: Whom I love

I trust summarily to see me well,
however poorly I wake up.
I weigh a hundred and a half.
I owe the laughter of my life
to motherly extravagance: sweet yearning, sage
advice, a little cold cash
in the worst of times, and earnest questions
which I answer blind.

In God I gloweringly trust.

I'm worth my weight in bedroom dust.

Stopped by Twilight

Forest shadows embark
on the half dark
of a boneground roadway:

blown, they sway
like dancing snakes.
The neighing brakes

assume a storm,
the air warm,
weighted with souls

from savage holes
back among the trees.
At one stark breeze

a moccasined shape
looms up to gape.
Groomed for terror,

tormented by our error,
I floor the gas
and as I pass . . .

Twang! Whoosh! Thwack!
Sitting Bull's back!

Admiral Shell

Who stands alone on the bridge of the Admiral's warship?
The Admiral stands alone, on his own bridge.
Who owns the ocean the Admiral gazes out on?
The Admiral owns the ocean, and the bridge.
Owning the bridge, and beginning to own the ocean,
others beyond the moon were in his eye.
Somewhere along, the ocean held his eye.
Under their names, he remembers the names of the stars.
Under his name, he is naming the bridge and the ocean.
Over the ocean he noses the bridge of the warship,
showing his face from the bridge of his posturing warship,
shelling the ocean, shaking the bridge, reloading.

Her Garden, His Dream

"Today? Today?" (Oh, close your face!)
and I rummaged out the trowels.
Overalled, we dug all day
and half the God damned night.
Yes. Flowers.

Nicked and knotted,
dirty, burnt,
you hope to Christ we did it right
and flop down on the bed.
Good night.

Now among crickets with my cheese and beer,
their wing-song fevered, drowsy, old,
and glad the lawn sends up its chill,
I cast about for Orion.

The air of midnight makes me think of thighs.
The full moon makes me think of thighs.
Thighs are the thousand stars I cannot name.
I am tired of casting about.

It is a queen-size, mine the smaller space.
I lay a hand upon your crotch—
your little snort, and then your deeper sleep.
And soon the springs have ceased to creak.
I drift.

To Pigweed. (Pigweed?) Pigweed!
I am Pigweed, wild, alive,
her stems within my stringy jaws—
the Goosefoot troops, my brothers all
beneath this law, all crawling in to root!

II

GONE LARKING

Lecture on Genesis

In the Beginning was the End
and the End was endless:
it begins like this.

It goes on:
in the End was the Beginning
which began to end
when it began.

Going over it again:
in beginning we begin
the End, in ending
the Beginning.

We begin to understand.

The End.

The Beginning.

The End.

The Terminal Longing

is to be so dead
that nothing but flat prose
can catch the feeling
and turn it
into something like
a poem. There are however
in its execution
risks peculiar to the monotone
it strives to capture, indeed
to reinforce. Rats for example
have been shown to shun
intercourse, even die of
hunger, in order to bear out
or break the backs of
certain theories, while
other recent studies
seem to indicate that
boy scouts high on sugar
make a poor job of crossing
the elderly, sometimes
pummeling and robbing them
at the impatiently honking
midpoint between
two congested sidewalks.
                              What this
all means to poetry today
tries our best minds. Strictly
speaking, metaphor does not move
mountains, nor are mountains
in the habit of moving
themselves, perhaps because
why should they move,

what is wrong with
where they are.
                    Pope
Leo once said to Attila
in apocryphal Latin the Hun
could only gnash at:
"Show me the dog's hair,
I will name you
it's kingdom." Poets today
know this sort of thing
intuitively, tamp down the core
and quick of it with flat
prose. So it is they catch
the feeling of being
dead, which is—as God
Himself might say—the way
it goes, folks, as
the poem flows.

Weeds

"Old rake, come out of your cellar hole!
Come out and pluck the weeds!"
A wicked eye the old woman had
but the old man held to his knees.

"Old cock," she crowed, "if ye don't come out
I'll be fetchin' ye wid me axe!"
But what of her blustering ways and all,
he'd had no heart attacks.

A bristling haze spun off the moon
and its broad light caught her full.
Her eyes in a knot she continued to cry,
"Come out, you sot, and pull!"

"I'm prayin' me prayers," he finally said
from the dark of his cellar hole.
"I'll make no bones, ye can pull 'em yourself,
for I'm set on savin' me soul."

The woman went into the cottage then
where she muttered a thing or two,
and took to her belly the last of the gin
and the last of the mulligan stew.

Out under the light of the moon again
with the skillet and carving knife,
she cried, "Pious old toad, if ye don't come out
you'll be leaving a very good wife!"

"Amen!" came the wondrous loud retort
from his hole down under the house,
"if it's malice ye mean the likes of me
you're beratin' a blameless spouse!"

The moon fell back from a leaden attack
of thickening, threatening clouds;
the old woman whacked with her skillet and knife;
the cottage crept into its shroud.

The old man came staggering up from his hole
with his head and his guts in his hands.
Now how was he ever to pluck her old weeds
when he could barely stand?

With her knife and skillet and iron will
the old woman followed him out,
and saw that he plucked every mother's son's weed
urged on by occasional clouts.

And when it was over she put him together
with spit and a smidgeon of clay.
"Go back to your cellar hole," said she,
"and pray if ye need to pray."

"I know what I need, I know what I am,"
he said in a quavering voice.
And the pair of them vanished forever from earth.
And the sun was inclined to rejoice.

No News from Suburbia

Bounding over
the roof tops
whelps clamped

at her dugs
(twelve
I counted) one more

at her tail
the great fiery
bitch blundered off

into blue space
the nails
flying out of

our houses
our children
asleep.

Too Together

for Robert Bly

You open your eye, I put my nose in,
and this weird thing happens!

My nose is a naked turkey pushing its face
into your crushed eye, which is a marshmallow!
An Eskimo kissing a peeled egg!

Suddenly we are in Miami drinking wine
under a beige umbrella!
Your fist knuckles into my groin,

my nose falls out of your eye,
we writhe on the ground!
The screaming, wheeling gulls

send us white messages of love from on high!
We learn love from our separate pains,
we love the mailbox, and the mayor's blue tennis shoes!

Oh we will share our future with the snail
of our insane son's latest nightmare!
We are two Howard Johnson clam rolls

filling the Sunday eternity of our mother faces!
We are foreign correspondents
covering the assassination of a pimp in western Nebraska!

We are two cockroaches cuddling in the fur of a mother grizzly
which is looking up at some stars that are tumbling like
      peachstones

painted with some phosphorescent substance!

We roll like Coke bottles over the mother tongue,
spitting our broken marbles into the mouth of the mother
      universe forever!

Poem Written on a Page Torn from My Notebook in Blank Innocence of Ceremony by One Earl Cook, 74, Mildly Hard of Hearing, Who Heartily Thrust it Then into My Face and Shouted, "You're a Poet, Eh? Here, Write Me a Little Poem."

Here's a wee poem for Earl Cook
who ripped this page from out my book
without my saying that he could.
Guess I could say 'tweren't truly good
of Earl to do my book so rude;
guess I could say it was damned crude
of him, in fact—but what the hell,
he don't hear much, but he means well . . .
Well, maybe I'd best modify
that last suggestion: It's no lie
Earl's in a friendly way with folks;
still he's one Cook whose broth revokes
the taster's joy of first full cup
by not subsiding sup by sup
but rather staying flush to rim
or overflowing, as the whim
betake him. What I mean by this
is nothing Earl should take amiss.
I like you, Earl, I really do;
nor would I say so weren't it true.
As to the tactless fact of you—
so full of Earl you miss my act
entirely—I could now impact
your wisdom with a toothy tract
upon both heels and topple you
as you stand and deliver (no shy oaf
in vein of words) the staling loaf
of Cook and Earl, Earl and Cook,

until that thick, toastworthy book
called *Earl Cook's Life* run out of slices—
(likewise spent, the body's juices)—
and they lay you out at last
in final deafness . . . But no! I'm past
such mad assaults on senior sports
whose ears are closed to such reports
as others would give on life around—
so here's your poem, Earl: one proud pound
of beefy thought so finely ground
you'll get it down with passing ease.
You'll grant as how it has no grease
and give me that it well agrees.
It's worth a picture, Earl. Say cheese.

Teachings of a Shadow to His Spirit

This is how you enter the sky:
eyes towards it, hands
straight up to tear the clouds,
knees at a slight bend, legs tensed
for a phenomenal lunge; then,
forget you're on the ground . . .

That's it! That's it! Mimic the birds!
Ceremony is a trick of earth . . .
Kick off your shoes, your socks,
all the skins that resist air!
Whooom! Ha*ha*! Dip! Climb!

The sun follows like an orange cow.

Kabir Studies the American Psyche

Between the outhouse and the insane asylum, the swing
          has put up a mind:
all back and forth the winding streets, millions of
          movies flicker on a white sheet—
double and triple features, even myopic Huns on
          skateboards, even the Bossa Nova—
and they never wind down.

Cannibals, catfish, campfires and chickens, even the
          wheeling monk with his spoon,
and the wet grass that stains the white trousers of
          Beethoven lovers,
and lice in the bag lady's hair:
friend, they open like flowers on the endless sheet,
and these films are completely uncensored.

Kabir stuck his head out the window of either the
          outhouse or the insane asylum
(Kabir will tell you the truth: one place was as dark
          as the other)
and grabbed himself a 15-second gander of all that;
then he slammed the window shut, jumped through it
          feet first,
and went and got him a job as a servant in a house
          on Main Street between 8th and 9th out in the
          old part of town,
where home movies continue to thrive amid screaming
          reminders
that it's *all maya, and it never winds down!*

*Note: Kabir is the revered 15th-century Indian mystic who left us a body
of mind-sweeping poetry in Hindi; it is not known how he came by his
impressions of America.*

The Cosmic Pundits Cheer Your Precious Act

You've barely read your contract for the act
when off they whisk you for your physical!—
then makeup, on through wardrobe, and now
all pinstriped and polished
in your foam and satin prop, you glide
through facile memory of lines
never written, you speak them
with serenely bursting heart,
and all who will
attend you well: Some weep, some
laugh, some sit down dumb.
                              You're dropped
right where you're going
unrehearsed
and ready for the Big Time!
Grace silence then, which savors
your restrained performance soundly—
with grand ovation in its only coin:
Silence for speech
we now of one voice praise you,
whom time now places well beyond time's reach.

The Bottom of the Bag

Bravely, the bottom held.
A hundred more of anything thrown in,
the whole thing lifted
by the sides,
still it held.
How strong it was!
How well it would contain
our own lives, when the time came.

Coming upon a woods
we caught a bear, a beaver
and a yodeler.
They all went into the bag.

When Beatrice gave birth to triplets
we put them in the bag.

We drove our Chevy to the bag,
it broke our hearts
but in it went.
The bottom held and held.

One day we were bored.
We brought our bag to the mayor.
The mayor sniffed it.

We said to Simon,
"Well?"
He said,
"Forget it."

By then the war had come
and we were into popcorn and late shows
and letting it all hang out.

Little by little
we forgot our bag.

Our bag grew lonely
with the weight of years,
with all our object sufferings and joys.

At last we put it out.
The trash man came and picked it up.
He wasn't all that careful,
some spilled out.
But most went with him,

And the bottom held.

Confession on a Tight Budget

I try resisting, but my hand says, "No!
You've got to write it down!" I say, "What is it?"
My hand says, "Who knows? Just get on with it!"

So here I am, the hand itself, such words
as it would say from me this moment,
and I am less than easy at the prospect.

That demon keeping all in check until
the words are ocean, and the waves are tall,
hurls an obscene guffaw and sounds the knell!

My droll hand ushers up a dreadful calm.
I surf the doldrums, and confide in awe
there's much about me that's outside the Law.

Tsunami Surfer's Psalm

The Lord is my surfboard, I shall not want
      small waves

He maketh me to stand up on tall combers

He giveth me a well-oiled outtasight bod
      blinding teeth and killer smile

He hath granted me to date four thousand
      three hundred and two unforgettable mountings
         and ridings and graceful beachings

Against all hours of waveless calm, when lonely
      surfers reel for want of balm, He hath loaded me
         chock full of sex appeal

Even now or at the hour of my—(Christ I hope not!)—death
      He doth suffer me to stand atop the ocean
         propped and primed, a pin-up of devotion

The Lord is my surfboard my nuance my rhythm
      I ride on the Lord—(Holy Jesus!)—for save after save

I am nothing in this moment but the pleasure of the Lord

Jesus Christ what a wave!

A Positive Mourning

Someone unlearned of sea or self
set sail on an angry tide.

He was as young as we are old
who stand all night on the slick stones
lashed with the blinding spray.

God knows we've a fair drop taken
for fellowship's sake in the raw hour,
though our eyes remain our eyes
and we all of us tell you this:

The ocean is our friend at times,
a grain of salt allows it.
He or his bones will one day find
a way through all the waters
and meet us at this place.

We make our prayerful stab at faith
that he is still alive, though he's surely dead.
Lord take our prayer with a full cup;
deliver us then to bed.

A Monk Gone Larking

I came alone into this grove
held by my own hand as it held
the grove before me. The asphalt

was at its shimmering pitch,
dead noon, when I sought respite here
from journeyman's bemusement

and stiff thumb. I parted
branches of oleander and stinkweed
to gain entry; then I nosed

among the pathway shrubs
till pine and honeysuckle deafened
my longing to be gone

swiftly over the highway. I found
this cool and modest trickle
of a stream, the towering oak

spread over it, and this mossy
scoop of stone which cups me
naked, my toes barely touching

the clean thread of water. Am I
happy? I don't know, don't
know. But am I sad? Oh, surely not.

It is a long way between
the coasts, and motorists dreamed all morning
my thumb would stop their hearts.

Very well, there's no hurry. Perhaps
the dusk will change me to an angel
visible on the soft shoulder

to some reckless nun whose love of Jesus
burgeons suddenly out of bounds
and brings her to an easy halt

beside me. So this is Ohio. Who
knows? Maybe Boulder
or Santa Fe is where she aims

her Chevrolet. Her face is boldly
shy and beautiful, her body
lovely to ride beside

in blue slacks and white cotton blouse,
her hilly hints of verdure cresting
softly under woven snow, the radio

booming "Okie from Muskogee"
as I pass her the blackberry brandy.
She takes a belt that's neither

greed nor daintiness and passes
back the bottle. Does she mind
if I smoke? Hell no,

go right ahead, do I have
any hemp, ha, ha? I do, ha ha.
Now the Chevy's on air jets five feet

above the highway, in perfect gear
to hold its lane and harmonize
with the singing wires strung

pole to pole on the loping
summer-velvet dusk. Let's
rob some banks, she says, her

girlish giggle filling me
like the tickle of crickets
on my dreaming stone. Why

not, I say, and will my body's
easeful rising from green moss
to sit my private self

down happily in the streambed trickle,
proclaiming lustily in song
my fairest praise of one sweet nun

before I rise again, shake dry, dress
and tread the underbrush
back to the edge of the open road,

halo at rakish tilt,
my thumb
a monk gone larking.

Moriarty's Nightly Sermon to Himself

Trust that your brain is scrambled.
Attend your half-assed sermon like a knight
knocked off his steed, the bouncer eyeing
as his echo rings: Last call!
Give up your stool, your very self,
and drag you from your social zoo,
you goddamned oafish, drunken hazard
lost to liberty for want of mind's good eye!

Well, with mind's bad eye, then, espy
the patience of that courtly buzzard
waiting for its fair share of you
one reeling block of ruffled gulf
from where you barely stand, your tepid squall
of gaseous sermon neighing
like a romp of phantom horses, the night
unpurposed but to watch you trampled.

III

IN FROGGING TIME

Love's Virgin

Praise Death! but leave a candle by for Love:
Love's virgin, in her cave, keeps costly love,
laying an altar cloth of emerald slime
over the sacrificial face of time
and lying there, the darkest hours of life,
liberal mistress, unobstructive wife
to white infinitudes of frozen space;
the dragon, dreaming, in its proper place.

The General's Will

1.
One thought, well paced, brings up
the sun, another
sends it down: the sort of day
a clean, commanding mind
puts on the world.

2.
I slog through bogs of déja vù,
the dawn horizon blood
to my angelic thirst for order,
essence of liberty,
anarchy dead!

3.
My troops catch fire,
they devour
their chocolate and move
like a cloud of murder
over the hill.

A Midnight Confidence

Before I bed with my own love
I skirt this last poem of the day
and pray that such a dressing up
were meet, at such a latened hour.

I pray the poem were woman such
she might have called me from a dream
dreamt in the passageways, and I
entering room on room reclined
with multitudes of who she was.

She scans me as I come along,
the walls so comfortingly close
I cannot dread my sanity
or strike a discord.
                    If I falter
under the thousand spells of darkness,
she will slip the threads that bind me—
breath of word, bed of line;
and her deathless eyes will shine me
home past midnight, like the sun.

The Big Banker

Banks are my beauty, currency my flow.
Frameworks of plain greed fluctuate. I feel
such vigorous incentive in my field

I eat the earth, I drink the sea, I grow
lustrous, electric, eelish each brief while
I ride the ocean Principal: I, soul

of governance, the secret truth, the hole
my colleagues all at last fall into. Smile
if you own me, smile if I've buried you, smile if I seem

arbitrary, stupid, grossly drawn
out over time accountable. I loan
anyone anywhere any amount, and some

assume my interest philanthropic, some
unbearable; but all at last break stone.
And I own banks. And I build more of same.

Soliloquy For Rough Beast

*The religious spirit can only be realized if the stage of development
of the human spirit which it expresses in religious form,
manifests and constitutes itself in its secular form.*

—Marx

*And what rough beast, its hour come round at last,
Slouches towards Bethlehem to be born?*

—Yeats

I love what lay down with a deadly end,
embraced that end, and was sated.
I love what insists it will die.
I hate loving
what does not exist, but the shadows seduce me
with their evanescent spite.
                I strike
such images from the mold of my maculate life
you would be starstruck, saints of old,
on brief re-acquaintance.
                Endlessness
dwells in the temporal seed
of every living man;
the egg of a woman glows against all ending;
yet, ye are redeemed, ye miserable dogs,
in the thrum and drum of the sundered minds
that move in chorus over the plains of death.

    Let us pray:
that the purse be never empty;
that notwithstanding, the purchase be made on time;
that the goods be true to their six-month guarantee;

that the golden retrievers of corporate boards
        be on the ball whenever the birds of appetite
                fall freshly dead into the dense brush
                        of the Gross National Product;
that praise be theirs who fill a house with holdings;
that hell be theirs whose doors are marked
        with the red X of insolvency;
that the erect tit of Mammon my Father erupt forever
        through the clamped teeth of those best able
                to fondle and suck.

Blessed be the poor, for they shall seek riches.
Blessed be the rich, for they shall resist all change.
Blessed be the range of my truth.

Let no man utter, the length and breadth of earth, the
        awesome lie:
I love what does not die!

Above the Attic Room

Jesus whose thundering hooves is those
is what I, waking, ask. And they are
not from dream, are a thing lives close, scuttling
matchstick feet along the ceiling's floorside.
Jesus the hour four a.m.
floats phosphorescent in my eye. Sleep
is a dead man, hoarse thought nag:
this is a lower trick, to be a sound
where darkness has the final say. But my voice
goes off, a limping rage, "You tiny bastard
up there, rattle someone else's timbers!
Else, show yourself and share the rent!"

Farewell to Angel Dog

for Luna, 1969-85

The dog remembers not to turn
suddenly out of a dog
into
a man, for example, or woman, because
dogs have good memories
for dogs, and dream
what dreams befit a dog,
and seem so utterly just dogs
that they *are* dogs,
is what they are.
How is it then I am
a man who turns
suddenly out of a man
into a dog, and dreams
dog dreams, and seems
just dog? Is it
the angel in me flies
foolishly out of me to be
free to be dog
or not be dog, free to avenge
my human horror of disdain
for all that is or is not
dog, yet likewise
free—somehow—free
to be or not to be
beyond a question
who I am,
or man or dog?

The Calling Home

This longing rose
and my voice was a wild woman writhing,
triumph of demons
sprung from tensed cords just awakened
by demons that thrashed in their sleep,
and I cried
"I am weeping
for freedom so boundless
no body stays to gawk or tremble . . ."

And when the wave passed
I tendered
my heart like a flower
that is the music the bee answers
for his queen,
all worlds in cycle . . .

Even deafness crawls out of its cave
when the demons go sailing
on the deep blue of the open sea
that is the silence love calls home.

The Blind Voyeur

Lovely, she loses
nothing in my eye,
nothing she loses

dress a blue swirl
of white flowers
flung to a far wall

nothing left on as she loses
nothing, nothing
in my eye

and dances till dawn
in her bright room,
alone

the whole dark night.

In Frogging Time

Frogs hibernate in slime,
rise to mild weather,
sing for sex,
get it
and go back under.

Going for frog you go
barefoot, cuffs
rolled, bucket, net.

Time in space, space in time:
the phrases lap
in languid symphony
round and round and round
your frogging mind.

Time
is the space
time occupies,
space
is the time
left over.

To catch a frog
be pure of space,
be light, be swift, be patient,
be on time.

Dear Annual Alumni Giving Program

Perhaps I am giving you something.
Perhaps I am giving you nothing.
Let me explain.

I've never owned a checkbook. I keep
a bit of cash on hand,
but mail is a poor vehicle
for that pure symbol, tempter
that it is.
And money orders seem so cold
between dear friends,
dear friend.

And so, the gift I send
is this small poem
that wants to say:
I give you something
if you say so, or nothing
if you say so. In either case,
this poem is yours.

May it surprise you
as it surprises me.
May it speed you on your journey
of all the old school needs,
a guide you might complaint to
when your dollar canoe seems
swamped, about to sink.
May it send your spirits
up or down,
whichever they prefer.

May you find you have taken millions
when you reach the counting shore.
And may you please write me
for money,
                    dear friend,
                         no more.

The Fugitive Painter

In some ways too estranged from life to bother trying to beat the rap, let alone run, this drunkie painter with long, slender fingers who recently strangled his future mother- in-law back of a kissing booth in Bar Harbor, Maine has nonetheless managed a move to Barcelona where he goes grubbily well with the piss-smelling cobbles and crusts of spit-roasted chicken sticking to the chin hairs of shawled, dusky shadows surreally related to something he has been after in his art from the beginning: the hint of a basic truth; but the authorities have traced him across five channels, from research on termites in Lima, Peru to an Italian bakery on the Thames where the Great Plague got its second wind, to a small African nation whose presidential elections are overseen by a clever Caucasian military intelligence man from Great Britain, and back to Bar Harbor, and back to Barcelona, their noses sucking up hundreds of erratic scents until the pissiest, booziest and least equivocally his leads them—along with his former future wife who is still hopeful his insanity is temporary and has flown from DesMoines to beg the authorities to use small bullets—to the base of an abandoned water tower just outside the city where, upon seeing them trudge epiphanally across a field of tall weeds towards him, he drops the stick with which he has been picking his toes, gets up and drawls to an imaginary playmate, "C'mon, Julio, let's go paint some donkeys."

Plan for the House

First, we will frame the space:
not with ink and hammer
or lines of stone

or vortex of
ideas
planed and notched

but as it comes
to us at night, an ocean
for the rolling floor

walls of wind
and over us
the years, and all

as even as our hearts'
first plan for this—
the space of us . . .

The devil take a crooked house!

Our level
        for these surfaces
                    is love.

La Bandera Contra Los Dragones

for Eugenie

The panting *hijo del chingado buey*
y su madrastra of the fallen ass
are kinds of *nada,* never meant to pass
that last inspection that might give us day,

but the inspecting angel *ya dormia*
y (pobre!) el planeta no sabia
que malas fueron las noticias
the separate days this pair began to crawl

towards marriage, and a graduated gall . . .
Give 'em the bird, *pues, piss* on their *malicias:*
your *via crucis* to some cold *capilla*
is *your* invention, and the varnished *silla*

on which you plunk your ass is *not* your world,
nor is it theirs, nor are you thus unfurled.

Of Soldiery and Sex

In the cold going off to war
his young eyes
swim
like sperm
in a gallon bowl,
                    civilian
        still
in his gait and garb
but given to mild heroics,
the hang of the fists, the turkey
gun, the mental wagers
won as his boots crunch snow;—
he shows his teeth to winter
birds, experiments with stealth
where the deer play close, and leaps
(to enliven the promise
he's made to women folk)
and clicks his heels to be free
of them, and earning them,
and on his own . . .

                    Come night
nine months a soldier
he earns his phantom bride,
his mother murmurs blessings
his sightly sisters cry
as he sings the bittersweet
sense of them to
sleep
beside his grave, and

                                    gives
                        his
                heat
to the luminous lust
all living heroes have
for one adoring one
among the women they would lay
down their lives for.

Economy of Ashes

Our lonliness lies always in the fact
we fail to trust each other to exist.
The dusk of failure is the dawn of grief,
in whose deep heart is found
reason for resolution, change, perfection—
impermanence surrounded by the light
of lasting clarity within, without
the hard, half-cocked or shuffling designs
of willful grandeur or humility
sentencing every act of us to death.

But who will mind the store if sane self-image
spreads its wings of crepe and gauze and goes
exploring the wild challenge beauty springs
suddenly on an empty screen forever?
Never mind—for hunger teaches us the dream
does not begin, end, or begin again, but only
carries on, a caste of passions
playing feasts of us.

                Shall we come feeding
out of the blue sky then, or fall back
wingless and damned by judgment's snapshots
of all our stricken postures? Oh,
swoop and swallow
what graces our desire has spawned!—
for there's no yesterday
we loved so well, nor a tomorrow
binding: only the now
both fabled and real . . .

Or should we drown in it
we'll dream once more of that despairing sea
upon whose scattered islands we embrace
all we did not know lost, it somehow like us
to forget—from dream to waking, death to birth—
that mind moves ever lifewise, like the Phoenix,
beyond the ashes of our time on earth.

The Dream of a Citizen Soldier on the Eve of His Execution

Knocked down, he rises and salutes.
The squad reloads, and cocks, and shoots again.
Again the one real bullet socks
him hard on the heart, he drops again, gets up
again, steadies himself, salutes.

The squad reloads, and cocks, and shoots.
The shapely bullets, all but five, are blank.
They fly to him, they find his heart,
he flies with them a few yards, lands,
relaxes, asks to be excused.

The squadsmen smoke a cigarette.
Some inhale deeply, some do not inhale,
yet each achieves a smoke ring in the air.
The executed man lights up,
leaks smoke, leans forward, lip-reads. Likes the joke.

He rises and salutes.
The squad reloads, and cocks, and shoots.
The shapely bullets, all but twelve, are blank.
Their belt is beautifully to heart.
He somersaults to footstand, and salutes.

The squad reloads and cocks and shoots.
Eight thousand rifles rock the sky.
The shapely bullets, all but one, break lead.
The little bees bring honey to his heart.
He hums. He sighs. He stands apart.
Salutes.

Détente

Sometimes I wonder
how a thought can capture
itself as I struggle to suggest
it exists at all, let alone
that it is my thought, even
as I think I'm thinking it.
That's the thing I don't like
about thoughts, they're so
vagrant, so snarky, so
stuck on themselves
they seldom give the thinker
a break. But here's what I
think: I think the thought
I'm thinking this moment
marries peace and agitation
in the faint bliss of détente,
even as I'm so foolish
as to go on thinking
I'm thinking it.

Late Reckoning

As words were all I had in mind
I chewed my pen to splinters while
the virgin page confirmed me blind

beyond the shadow of a guile
to what I'd call my "winter's tale"
had I the wits to summarize

the volume of her spring-fed eyes
which served me ice for my fair lies.
As I go down inside myself

on absolution's mildewed quest
I hug a loaf of grief so fresh
it feeds the flesh of time, the restive

dream of ever being, robust and endless.

Urgent

Say only the words
lure you onto a mind field, you
dig maniacally for raw proof
someone exists, you don't care who.

Somewhere a bell, as epic
as the spade ten times the size of you,
tolls a blend of mourning and warning
for no reason, for the digger.

Cellars open up, bones begin to come
clean, shades brush your eyes
importantly. But when, in the crisis of
sweet labor, someone calls

from the other room, be glad
there's a world that breaks you down
in worlds of self. Life is always
about itself. The dead must wait.

A Prayer for Everyone

Blessed are the absent, for they are not here;
Blessed are the near at hand, for they would seem to be;
Blessed are the saved and the damned, for both are born to blessing;
Blessed are the best and the worst, the wisest, the most foolish;
Blessed are the fallen, the risen, the reverent, the ghoulish;
Blessed are the good, the bad, the having and the had;
Blessed are the graves of the living, the mansions of the dead;
Blessed are the wretched, the sovereign, the suffered, the expelled;
Blessed, all the realms we remember, realms we forget;
Blessed, every landfill, every hole;
Blessed, the souls in heaven, the souls in hell;
And blessed the beginning and the end;
And blessed, ever blessed, thrice blest, the unbegun and neverending;
And blessed, ever blessed, the blest and the unblest:
May all find rest.

IV

THE GREEN TIP OF LAND

As It Begins

Let it end
as it begins
a pale green flash

in that no-ness
of an eye
calmly watching

with potential
wit and wonder
over all nothing.

Let it never
end at all
that never was

before it was
because
why would it.

Let every speck
by which it is
diminished

every second of
its being make
the great leap back

to being.
Let it be
and be not.

Let it ever
begin. Let it end
as it begins.

The Men of Moss

"I am the king's confessor: kiss my ass
and I'll arrange your earthly paradise.
Pass me an apple, at your spirit's ease,
and I'll inscribe you, that it won't erase.
But hear! resist my sovereign pleasure's pose,
my parchments must exclude you from their praise,
and all who love the king must love you less
than snakes that lowly wind without his lease."

"Levelly sounded!" shout the Men of Moss:
all gather stones to drive the demon ruse,
railing and bleeding, back to his true face,
and out of the affairs of common force . . .

Now, as men dance to drums of ended crisis,
their women drone, "The way we sigh, oh, useless."

Riding Out

Feeling the rawhide wits gone taut within him
the generous new cowboy calls to order
his whole shebang of average emotions
brands 'em with one quick flash of white hot eyes
and tells 'em go and graze from hell to heaven.

High in the saddle, sleep was never more
precisely surgical: the solar brain
sings its assumptions to the lunar heart
whose humdrum approbations bridge the gap
between the blood and lungs, and leave him coping.

The kinfolk take it cleanly on the chin
benches of grief and hammocks of reflection.
The decent minister has urged him home
blessing his bones away to higher fiction.
But finer tumbleweeds he's never known.

His last religion is the cowboy one.

Interrogating the Prophets

There is a sleep
on which the prophets graze
and amble, ringing
their cowbells of complete
instruction, rousing
the dim remains of
memory
toward peaks of nothing
new.
      Then down and down
to morning's valley
from those star-hung
heights, they slowly turn
ten thousand times —
before we teach them
what to tell us,
when we ask them
as they stand there
where they are.

Father Flynn and the Feather Man

Are your vestments very heavy, Father Flynn?
For feathers would you trade them in?
Would you trade them in, Father Flynn?

Fifteen dark years out of acolyte grace . . .
(God! mollify the dog in that frothing face,
he shakes as his fist shook then!)
. . . and what is sin now, Father Flynn?

I remember swelling glands,
tendons stretched like rubber bands,
when you barked your stand against erection:
a reckless stand oh that one, Father Flynn!
for Grail and God a bollix of a win!
One thought the thing that dangled
didn't mean to be at all
but the devil, and his wife thrown in!

Own up now, old Father Flynn,
how many little friggers have you flogged?
How many, many dog-descended hands
have been barred by *your* rod,
Father Flynn, Father Flynn,
from fiddling that full-fledged sin?

And sniffing, always sniffing up the saints!
Still, you stay on the stray side of death,
and elevate your host
and invoke your Holy Ghost—
well, your coast is clear now,
Father Flynn, Father Flynn,
the Feather Man's about to figure in.

By the by-view of your eye,
good bye,
good bye, Father Flynn.

I'd intone a *maledicat*, Father Flynn,
      if you hadn't only almost done me in.
      Now, instead, I toast your cheer,
      an enjoyable last year
      and an afterlife among the cherubim.

      You treated me to consciousness of death.
      You lettered it in black upon my soul.
      You said, "There is no way
      (here today and gone today)
      to appeal a sentence to the devil's hole."

So, open up your ear, Father Flynn,
it is time, I must confess:
that the weight of wine
on your holy breath
is the closest to death I've ever been,
Father Flynn,
the closest I've ever been.

Then, heavy hung your breath, Father Flynn,
and heavy hang your vestments, Father Flynn,
but the Feather Man has measured you
for wings, Father Flynn,
and where and what and how
is sin now, Father Flynn,
Father Flynn . . .
Father Flynn . . .
           Flynn . . .
              Flynn . . .

On Their Behalf Whom Thou Hast Granted Grace

Grant us Thy grumble, and restrain Thy grace,
O Thou Which Sitteth on the Grand Around:
Thy favored tote Thee by the bleeding pound
(And Thou art rare enough, in any case)
Under the hungry eyes of Sinful Sam
And Unbelieving Betty, who, beside
Themselves with lust for some of Thy sweet hide,
Savagely bite their chair legs, dreaming *Lamb* . . .
Why canst Thou not, O Ultimate Repast,
Pursue an open season on *all* souls,
Instead of stuffing hemlock in the bowls
Of just those many who offend Thy caste?
For Thine is the vast, and dark, and empty roar
That raiseth man to sainthood's lowest floor.

The Abbot's Depression

Prayer lights the way to nothing on the table
but what the guidelines for good Lenten struggle
specifically allow: a bowl of cotton,
a lacquered ear of clack and yellow corn,
one fig upon the verge of going rotten,
then three sips each from the communal horn
whose contents are a bitter mystery
brewed by the abbot in his private cistern.

His seven monks are silent by profession,
plausibly introspective, well established
in sequiturs, in rakes and hoes and bushels,
in bold delineations of the light
that shines from any mortal at the threshold
of high encounter; yet, who feel the bite
before the snake has slithered into vision,
eschewing so its dizzying excretion.

To each his midnight, and their solemn snoring
unmasks the shadow of an abbot poring
over the mists of his own spitting image
glittering in complexities of void
whichever way he turns, and towards whose grimace
a sanity of rhythm is deployed,
constraining him to dance the ides of madness
on menstrual floors, in frames of abbacy.

In Loving Memory of Food and Drink

for Ray Zarate, high priest

Arriving as we do—drunk and inspired,
certainly loving something: air, perhaps,
or water, or women's thighs, white lightning, wheat—
we owe our sensuous eyes to the light-year priest
who sacrificed a yearling in our names
and eased us sideways out of hungry times,
drawing the wine that goes so well with flesh
from oaken barrels, off spigots of sculpted bone
bravely abandoned (he said) by some walking saint
starved for the love of God, some years ago . . .

Stuffed bellies and sumptuous brains assign us now
to a heaven unburdened hearts allow to be:
we worship whatever walks, or waves, or washes
the warm terrain, on which we toast our priest.

Mystery Brief

Between the pomp and intonation
of the priest at his table
and the silvery babble of the wee babe
behind me in the back pew,
the angels of the sacred apse
can barely keep from tittering
in shades of newspun gold.

The choir suddenly kicks in;
the baby nails the key at once
and amps to tripled volume.

For one dark second I weigh
my abstract state of mere apostasy
against the sublimely palpable:
I am transported!

"What a synchrony of voicings!"
I rejoice within my silence,
and rise past reason like a wraith.

Thus I proclaim the mystery of faith.

A Candid Scribble As the Choir Soars

Singing out roundly, sounding, I begin
between disinterest and profound intent
to limn those fundamental first fast thoughts
fired from cannon mounted on the docks
of that colossal boatyard, my fleet mind,
where sweet and sour, sparse and sumptuous, bind
the comers, goers, and all in between
with elemental, evanescent twine
such that the bond dissolve as it is made,
that craft and craft might calibrate the shade
to their own likings, and adjust the sun
for scarcely any blisters as they run
the channel, or sit calm in port, keeping
the God's-eye of their ardent dream from weeping
for want of conscious effort not to lose
perspective, as they parse their lines and choose
the heart by which they'll sink this very second,
or stay afloat and sense where they are beckoned—
toward house of fabric or tent of stone;
and go or not, all reckonings their own.

Hands Feeling for a Blind Date

Shyly the hands begin to leave the body
to start their light year's journey toward the body
that inspires them to reach out.

Slowly they make their way
to the flesh-limned spirit couched a mile away,
hands that tingle with imagined fullness.

Eons later the hands settle down like feathers
on shoulders, arms, breasts, thighs, as the other
signals welcome, or not. Always

there's something worth the risk—some riff
so transcendent of the pale and cautious life,
it calls the heavens down to earthy days.

The hands go out in quest of body,
which houses spirit. How the hands return
is for embodied spirit to discern.

My Lazy Voice

Because I could not fall
easily down out of the sky,
I threw my lazy voice away;
it fell through emptiness and light,
through seamless void and teeming rush,
till it alighted on a lake
it liked enough, and there it stayed.

I came to miss it quietly.
I thought to call it back to me.
Of course I couldn't, don't you see.
And so, I climbed the whole way down.

My journey found me by a lake.
The only dragonfly around
makes passes as I part my lips
as if to speak to it. I don't.
Because of this we are fast friends.

Out on the lake, sound asleep
on a small splash of sunlight,
my lazy voice is all I hear . . .

Deep in the wellspring of the ear
lake upon lake of wood-ringed joy now fill me!

For the Stones of Mexico

Stones are my countrymen. I cherish more
the pace of conversation in these hills
than I have love for all the congregation
acrawl on that night-thimbled town.

                                     Leave me alone.
My liquor is the things I'm bound to say.
Don't worry if I say them to a stone.
You were not soon to hear them, anyway.
And, anyway, I keep them to myself.
The stones I know are deaf, and, though their hearts
are perfectly in order to receive
the storm of words a primitive might speak,
I know the meaning of unparted moss
and mind my syllables.

                             This man that talks
in awkward cadences of five sore feet
is sometimes an embarrassment to me,
but he is taking lessons from the stones,
and I am halfway hopeful he might learn
their lighter tongue . . .

                           So merciless is whim,
it ministers to no clean, silent time.
He thinks I must return with him to town.
He is for congress. I am for the stones.
My only message, from the stones to him:
here is your foreign country. I. Alone.

Harboring the Despised

As I was coming down with death
I drank hot rum with honey. Drunk,
I walked out to asses the wealth
of one late night in Mexico.
The air was in its beauty and
the stars stayed doglike at their posts.
I played a lizard trick and stood
deathstill, and drank the garden in
until the bronchial earth could turn
faint sweetness into fire and drug
my senses further. Then a walk
was what I wanted, so I walked.
Midway, the mile-long cave of trees
between my cottage and the bridge
turned in its utter darkness on
a band of star-mad dogs that had
been cowards all their daylight lives
and I, grown up to beat my eyes
with branches from the tree of fear,
shot blind roots down and sprouted rags.
This lockjawed mortal, mocking tree
and beggar in my darkened brain,
fed those dogs a food of broken
light! They marveled at their master!
I lay down dead and they began
my last good meal without me. Well:
the early wood man on his beast
would find me disembowelled and shake
his head. I was his customer
and he the bringer of pine fires
he had cut out of the high hills
beyond our rust-gowned roof tiles. So

it went that night that had begun
so simply in my ailing lungs.
Slowly I backed away from all
the dogs intended, throwing stones
my eyes invented, swallowing phlegm
and almost drunk again. There
is no sequel to this story,
which is a true one. I returned
to more hot rum, built up the fire
and by it ground my useless teeth.
Towards dawn a human strangeness stalked
and stoned me. I fell by the river.

An Old-Country Fellow

So, they would never ask of him to leave,
nor would he leave; nor could he well believe
they'd want him gone, but only to go on
ablathering, an atavistic gnome
old as the centuries that bless the shadowed
cervices of stone with moss, a meadow
in his own right, all inwardly afire, ten
thousand tonguely shadings painting him
angelic warden of the face of earth,
his own face knolled and furrowed to full worth,
an old-country fellow—for whose clear memories
of green-creatured nights wrapped in outlandic mist
the children of his descending star would sit
frozen behind their eyes, their helpless bodies
held in his arms of pipe smoke, the pure song
of his ancient heart's most fondly rendered words
whisking their souls away to better worlds,
to wider, wilder days . . .
                        But here, the sun
might rise and set without a single smile
stealing between the grownups and their bread,
and these (though good to him, as was the rule)
thought him a queer old lad, and wished him dead.

Pornographic, for Nathaniel Hawthorne

After the flash of naked trunk
                              (the towering
birch being flesh toned, ruggedly
puerile to his moon-
muddled eyes, and all the gawking
goblins of the night wood
whacking bush, battering mulch
in an orgasmic frenzy)
                              he found
himself prodigiously erect, as
centuries before had his, say, great great great great
grandfather, Jonathon Therefore, early
American driver of stakes
for burnings for a living, on much
the same sort of a night
in a wood so wild and like
this wood

he could hear the witch's football
fell prone and throbbed and came

to his senses

cursing the new generation
its genius and black magic

he hated the woods!

The Marriage Thorn

In the crucial beginnings of love the thorn ought flush
good blood from both the beneficiaries,
each to have theretofore decreed undying
libations of spirit and flesh and frequent potluck
unto the wellspring maintenance of the other
that neither, under duress of judicious romance
and its inevitable offspring, bring a quarrel
to the table of state whereat they feed their faces,
nor to the bed of origins, their fortunes
having made one vast cover against hard times,
unsolvable dreams, all shades of metaphor,
and every whim construed by lonely genius
to have begun to arrive at a holy truth
outside of perfect union; therefore go,
you whom the thorn has proved to each other's perfection,
a lesson in two-as-one, a clockwise biography
of fruits and leisures and pleasurable labors,
and be invisible among the tribe that creatures
silence with its moribund oration:
Lessen at least   the flame's ambivalence
by which we shadows of creation dance!

So

for Ray Amorosi

They said, "Seals, dancing
seals and . . . bears . . .
yes bring the bears!"

Mismeasuring,
my people—
what long lines of praise

wait outside
the main cathedral door . . .
Here, on my little farm,

I snore
long into day
the garden gone

to weed and worm,
caring
only for broad sweeps

across the waking hour . . .
(young gentleman Jack
born Thomas Francis

filling the blanks in
as he dances,
dodging flowers) . . .

Abridgement follows
Me through airs:
What seals? What bears?

It breaks my heart
the hope
the visceral ruin

so here I am
with my poem
fool at the funeral.

Mud Feast

for H.G.

The fever raged and ate his name,
this bard on a Quest in the pitch of night.
The ground erased his sodden sense
of step by step slogging along it,
assuring him he wasn't sure at all.
He sought some edge of the edgeless plot
he must create now for the sake of waking,
for white moths by the millions made him shiver.
How he had come to this nowhere from nowhere
discernible, seemed ample cause to weep
or laugh, to bark or mutter oaths,
or even gather footnotes for the dense rant
he would compose, once he'd composed himself.
He'd risen an inch, a foot, perhaps a yard
above the rain-bombed path that snaked the woods.
He walked on air, though only mud made sense,
the sluck and slosh of gravitas such thoughts
as he'd be testing now, if he weren't dreaming,
and if the thousand questions posed him slyly
by shrewd and wakeful beings of the wood
did not instill in him to crave mud more
than any makeshift, dreamtime scroll of air
around his feet. He only had to get there
before they'd know he had no way of knowing
where he was going, though he'd heard the drums.
The feast they'd laid to celebrate his coming
was covered with bright laurel, till he'd come.

100

When You're Out

When you're out in a lifeboat a man
eats himself, as if to say
I am tired of surviving
and being of sound mind select
from this limited menu
my own body
after so many days on the ocean;
but then you mistake him
for someone who never left land, someone
so close to his children
he never grew old, or the least bit
hungry, or heard
the ocean, its eyes on his door, murmur
Come, come away, come and marry . . .
and you shake off your fool's dream,
you bend
toward the green tip of land.